YOUR KNOWLEDGE HAS

Bibliographic information published by the German National Library:

The German National Library lists this publication in the National Bibliography; detailed bibliographic data are available on the Internet at http://dnb.dnb.de .

Imprint:

Copyright © 2018 GRIN Verlag
Print and binding: Books on Demand GmbH, Norderstedt Germany
ISBN: 9783668696242

This book at GRIN:

https://www.grin.com/document/423537

Aaron Rababaah

100 questions and answers for object-oriented programming (OOP) in C++

A comprehensive introduction from simple to advanced topics

GRIN Verlag

GRIN - Your knowledge has value

Since its foundation in 1998, GRIN has specialized in publishing academic texts by students, college teachers and other academics as e-book and printed book. The website www.grin.com is an ideal platform for presenting term papers, final papers, scientific essays, dissertations and specialist books.

Visit us on the internet:

http://www.grin.com/

http://www.facebook.com/grincom

http://www.twitter.com/grin_com

American University of Kuwait
Department of Computer Science and Information Systems

100 Q/A for OOP in C++

By

Dr. Aaron R. Rababaah, Ph.D.

April 23, 2018

0. What is OOP?
Object-Oriented Programming is a computer programming methodology/paradigm which is bio-inspired based on objects which constitute its fundamental building blocks as opposed to procedural programming which is based on procedures. OOP main elements: Encapsulation, Abstraction, Inheritance and Polymorphism. The elements of OOP will be explained in details and demonstrated in various parts of this tutorial.

1. What is a class?
The blueprint of an object, it defines (specification and implementation) object's states and behaviors.

```
//--------------- Point.h ---------------
class Point{
private:
    double x;
    double y;
public:
    void setX(double x);
    void setY(double y);
    double getX() const;
    double getY() const;
};

//-------------- Point.cpp --------------
void Point::setX(double x){
    this->x = x;
}

void Point::setY(double y){
    this->y = y;
}
double Point::getX() const{
    return x;
}
double Point::getY() const{
    return y;
}
```

2. Class vs. Struct
- Members (data and functions): class = private by default, struct = public by default.
- Access-specifier of base class / inheritance: class = private by default, struct = public by default.

3. What is an object?
An object is a single instance of a class; it is created by invoking the constructors of the class. Class exists in source temporal scope and objects exist in run-time temporal scope.

```
#include "Point.h"
```

```
int main(){
    Point p0;   // Point is the class, p0 is the object
    return 0;
}
```

4. Define abstraction in software in general

In computing, abstraction means separating concepts from details through a hierarchy of layers. Examples:

- A bit as an abstraction of a hardware electrical signal
- A variable name is an abstraction of a memory location
- A data type is an abstraction of a memory representation scheme by a compiler
- A function call is an abstraction to the actual detailed code implemented in the body of the function

5. Define data abstraction

- Creating a structure that defines a complex data type and legal operations on it. The design makes the interface of the data and operations accessible but hides the actual implementation of them.
- Example: a List class can choose to implement the container of the data elements as an array or as a linked list. This container is kept hidden from the user interface but public interface is provided to element read/write operations.

6. Define process abstraction

- Separating the process (method, procedure, function, subroutine or subprogram) signature/prototype from the detailed actual definition and implementation, so that the user is not concerned with how the process is implemented but rather how to use it.
- Example: a method is defined to sort a list of elements and can be implemented using insertion sort or selection sort and the only thing the user has to worry about is how to call it.

7. What is encapsulation?

- It is a mechanism to package the data and its operations inside one structure
- It is a data protection mechanism to dictate the way data is accessed (read/write)

8. What is information hiding?

The internal representation and implementation of an object is hidden from users. This concept encompasses: data abstraction, process abstraction and encapsulation.

9. Define inheritance

A mechanism for code reuse and independent extension of the base class. Example:

```
//--------------- Point3D.h ---------------
#include "Point.h"
class Point3D : Point{
private:
    double z;
```

```
public:
    void setZ(double z);
    double getZ() const;
};

//--------------- Point3D.cpp ---------------
void Point3D::setZ(double z){
    this->z = z;
}
double Point3D::getZ() const{
    return z;
}
//--------------- main.cpp ---------------
#include "Point3D.h"
int main(){
    Point3D p0;
    P0.setX(1.1); // defined in base class
    P0.setY(2.2); // defined in base class
    P0.setZ(3.3); // extended in derived class
    return 0;
}
```

10. Define polymorphism
- A mechanism that works in hierarchical inheritance where a certain behavior when invoked can have different forms based on the called function of the derived class.
- Example: a base class Animal defines "move" and "makeSound " functions ;a derived class Dog redefines the two functions to walk and bark respectively using the same function names in the base class, where as a Bird class redefines the two functions to fly and chirp.
- Polymorphism requires that functions in base class to be defined as "Virtual" so derived classes can redefine them.
- Virtual functions are bound dynamically at run-time whereas other functions are statically bound at compile time.

11. What are accessors ?
- They are the functions in the public interface that provide accessibility to the private data members for "read" operations.
- Example: see the getX, getY functions in the Point class.

12. What are mutators?
- They are the functions in the public interface that provide accessibility to the private data members for "write" operations.
- Example: see the setX, setY functions in the Point class.

13. How to write inline functions?
- If a function member is defined entirely in the class specification body (typically in .h header file) then, it is considered as an in-line function.

- Example: see the setZ function in the following example of Point3D class.

```
//---------------- Point3D.h ---------------
#include "Point.h"
class Point3D : Point{
private:
    double z;
public:
    void Point3D::setZ(double z){    // in-line function
        this->z = z;
    }

    double getZ() const;
};

//--------------- Point3D.cpp ---------------
double Point3D::getZ() const{
    return z;
}
```

14. How to do inline functions work?

- In inline functions, there is no function calls, the compiler replace every instance of their calls in the code with the body of the function saving the overhead associated with the function call mechanism.
- "inline" keyword can be used to specify a function as an inline.

15. What is public interface?

- Is a set of public functions defined in the "public:" section in the class body. This section provides the data accessibility of read/write operations as well as other service functions.
- Example: see the "public" section in Point class. We can add another service function that prints the data members x and y to the stdout as follows:

```
void print(){ cout << " X-coordinate = " << x << endl << Y-
coordinate = " << y << endl; }
```

16. What are private functions?

- They are functions defined in the "private" section of the class body where they are only visible to the class itself; They are used when the class needs to some internal functions that the user do not need to know about and they are typically helper functions that help other public functions.
- Example: suppose that in the Point3D function we need a function that will generate a random id# for the current object and we want to hide this function from the user so whenever a random ID is needed other functions in the class can automatically call this function:

```
void Point3D::randID(){
```

```
id = 1000 + rand() % (9000);
}
```

17. Define access modifiers
- Private: the section in the class that is only visible to the class it self
- Protected: the section in the class that is visible to the class and to its derived classes
- Public: the section in the class that is visible to all: class, derived classes and outer world.

18. Define state, data member, attribute, property
- They all refer to one thing, that is, the data fields that provide data specification for the class.
- Example: see the data members defined in the "protected:" section below.

```
class Point{
private:

protected:
    double x;
    double y;
    int id;
    double size;
    void randID();
public:

};
```

19. Define function, method & behavior
They all refer to the same thing, the means of modeling how the object can operate and behave. While data members model states and attributes, functions model actions, operations and behaviors.

20. What is class specification?
The entire class body where every data member declarations, function members prototypes, constructors, accessors mutator prototypes and other elements of class declaration; all of these are typically kept in a header file ".h" apart from the implementation file of the class ".cpp".

21. What is class implementation?
It is typically kept in a separate file apart from class specification. In the implementation file, all functions declared in the class specification section/file are defined including the constructors, destructor, accessors, mutators and other service functions.

22. Write the simplest class possible that does nothing.
    class MyClass{ };

23. What is an instance of a class?
- It is an object instantiated from a class. An instance of a class is created at runtime using one the available constructors. By setting its states/attributes/data members it becomes a specific instant/object of the class.
- Example:

```
//--------------- main.cpp ---------------
#include "Point3D.h"
int main(){
    Point3D p0;  // p0 is an instance of the class Point3D
    p0.setX(0.0);
    return 0;
}
```

24. Define instantiation
- To create a new instance (object) of a class. Only when you instantiate an object, then you can use it and communicate with it.
- Example:

```
//--------------- main.cpp ---------------
#include "Point3D.h"
int main(){
    Point3D p0;      // instantiating the object p0 from the class
Point3D
    p0.setX(0.0);  // using/communicating with the class
    return 0;
}
```

25. What is a message?
Objects interact with each other using messaging which is simply calling each other's functions and receiving/causing the desired response.

26. What are constructors?
They are special functions exits in the public section of the class used to instantiate and create new instances/objects of a class. The general characteristics of them include:
- They do not have a return type
- They have the exact name of the class
- They must be defined in the public section

27. What are constructor types and their purposes?
- Default constructor: called in two situations, when declaring an object without initialization and when explicitly calling the default constructor function.
- Overloaded constructor: called when the user wants to create an object and sets some or all of the data members of the class.
- Copy constructor: called when the user has a previously created object and want to copy it to a new second object by passing the object reference to the copy constructor of the new object.
- Example: see (Q32).

28. What happens if you do not provide any constructor to a class?
The system automatically provides:
- A default constructor that will create a new instance of the class but with uninitialized data members
- A copy constructor that does a shallow copy but not deep copy. See the question on shallow copy (Q70).

29. What are distinguishing characteristics of default constructors?
- No parameters or all defaulted parameters in its signature.
- Example: see (Q32).

30. What are distinguishing characteristics of overloaded constructors?
- One or more parameters in its signature.
- Example: see (Q32).

31. What are distinguishing characteristics of copy constructors?
- Only one parameter in its signature
- The parameter must be of its class type
- The parameter must be passed by reference
- Example: see (Q32).

32. What are destructors?
A destructor is a special function member of a class designed to execute the required code when the object is about to be destroyed. One important task under destructors is the dynamic memory de-allocation.
Example: for constructors and the destructor:

```
//--------------- Point.h ---------------
class Point{
private:
    double x;
    double y;
    int* connectedTo;      // array of IDs keeps track of point ids
connected to this.
    const int MAX_CONN; // max num of points to be connected to this.
public:
    Point();   // default constructor
    Point(double, double, int*);      // overloaded constructor
    Point( Point& p );    // copy constructor
    ~Point();  // destructor
    void setX(double x);
    void setY(double y);
    double getX() const;
    double getY() const;
};

//--------------- Point.cpp ---------------
void Point::setX(double x){
```

```cpp
        this->x = x;
}
void Point::setY(double y){
        this->y = y;
}
double Point::getX() const{
        return x;
}


double Point::getY() const{
        return y;
}
Point::Point(){ // default constructor
        MAX_CONN = 8;
        x=0.0;
        y=0.0;
        connectedTo = new int[MAX_CONN];
}
Point::Point(double x, double y, int* p){   // overloaded constructor
        MAX_CONN = 8;
        this->x = x;
        this->y = y;
        connectedTo = new int[MAX_CONN];
        for(int i=0; i<MAX_CONN; ++i) connectedTo[i] = p[i];
}
Point::Point( Point& p ){   // copy constructor
        MAX_CONN = 8;
        x=p.x;
        y=p.y;
        connectedTo = new int[MAX_CONN];
        for(int i=0; i<MAX_CONN; ++i) connectedTo[i] = p.connectedTo[i];

}

Point::~Point(){ // destructor
        delete [] connectedTo;
        connectedTo = NULL;
}
```

33. In function members, can the parameter names match the names of the data members?

- Yes they can but, the pointer "this->" must be used to access the class data members.
- Example: see the function setX in (Q32).

34. What is sub, derived, child, inheriting class?

- All of these terms refer to the same thing that is, a class that extends and reuses a previously designed class. The old class is the parent/super/base class and the new class is child/sub/child class.
- Example: see (Q9).

35. What is super, base, parent, inherited class?
See (Q34).

36. What is "friend" modifier for standalone function?

- "friend" modifier grants public access privilege to an entire other class or an external function defined outside the class that belongs to another class or a global function.
- Example:

```
//--------------- Point.h ---------------
class Point{
private:
public:
     friend void reset(Point3D& p);
};
```

```
//-------------------- main.cpp --------------------------
void reset(Point3D& p){
     p.x = 0;   // private members accessed by a friend function
     p.y = 0;
}
```

37. What is "this"?

- A private constant pointer that points to the current instance of a class and only can be accessed by the class itself.
- Example: see (Q32).

38. How do you make a class member friend of another class?

```
//----------------- Point.h ---------------
#include "PHelper.h"     // needed for the "friend" statement
class Point{
private:
public:
     friend void PHelper::reset(Point& p);
};
```

```
//------------------------------ PHelper.h ------------------------
```

```
class Point;    // forward declaration if "Point" type is needed
here
class PHelper{

private:
public:
    void reset(Point& p);
};
```

```
//------------------------- PHelper.cpp --------------------------
#include "Point.h"
// 1) required since the function reset accesses its members
// 2) "PHelper.h" is already included in "Point3D.h" no need to
include it here

void PHelper::reset(Point& p){
    p.x = 0;
    p.y = 0;
}
```

39. What is a friend class?
- Class A can grant Class B an access to all of its content including the private, protected and public sections by declaring it as a friend.
- Example:

```
//---------------- Point.h ----------------
#include "PHelper.h"    // needed for the "friend" statement
class Point{
private:
public:
    friend class PHelper;
};
```

```
//------------------- PHelper.h --------------------------
#include "Point.h"
```

```
//------------------- PHelper.cpp --------------------
// All functions have access to private, protected and public
sections of Point class.
```

40. What are virtual functions and why they are needed?
- It is a mechanism for dynamic function call binding in a hierarchical inheritance, also called polymorphism. Se (Q10) for a general example.
- If a function member of a base class is needed to be overridden in a derived class, then it should be made as "virtual" in base class, so in run-time it is bound dynamically based on the type of the object.

- Example:

```
//--------------- Point.h ---------------
class Point{
private:
   double x;
   double y;
public:
   virtual void print();
};

//--------------- Point.cpp ---------------
void Point::print(){
   cout << " X = " << x << "\t" << " Y = " << y << endl;
}

//--------------- Point3D.h ---------------
#include "Point.h"
class Point3D : Point{
private:
    double z;
public:
    void print();

};

//--------------- Point3D.cpp ---------------
void Point::print(){
   cout << " X = " << x << "\t" << " Y = " << y << "\t" << " Z = " << z
   << endl;
}
```

41. Define static binding
It occurs at compile time in function calls resolution in a hierarchy of inheritance if the functions members in base classes are not declared as "virtual". See (Q40) if "virtual" key word is removed.

42. Define dynamic binding
It occurs at run time in function calls resolution in a hierarchy of inheritance if the functions members in base classes are declared as "virtual". See (Q40).

43. How does object slicing work?
- It occurs when an instance of child class is assigned to an instance of a parent class, since child class potentially contains more data members; the extra data members will be sliced of lost in the process, hence the name.

- Example:

```
//-------------------------------- main.cpp ----------------------------
Point p1D;
Point3D p3D;
P3D = p1D;      // object slicing
```

44. Compare function overloading vs. overriding vs. redefinition

- *Overloading*: defining multiple function using the same function name but with different parameter list ether in type or number. In classes, the overloaded constructor is an example where you can have many constructors with different parameter list signatures.
- *Redefinition*: if a base class non-virtual function is redefined in a derived class, it is called redefined and it is statically bound.
- *Overriding*: Redefinition: if a base class virtual function is redefined in a derived class, it is called overridden and it is dynamically bound.

45. Compare early binding vs. late binding
See (Q41 & Q42).

46. What are pure virtual functions and how do you specify that?

- A mechanism that mandates all functions defined this way in the base class to be overridden in the derived class. The pure function has no implementation code in the base class, it is only stated as a prototype = 0;
- Example: go back to (Q40) and modify as follows:
  - In Point.h: virtual void print() = 0;
  - In Point.cpp: remove the function "print" from the file.
  - In Point3D class: this class MUST override the function "print".

47. Define abstract classes

- A class that can only be derived (inherited from) but cannot by instantiated (no objects can be created from it)
- A class that defines at least one pure virtual function is an abstract class.

48. Define multiple inheritance

- A derived class can extend/inherit from multiple base classes which allow the derived class to have more than one parent and inherit their functionality.
- Example:

A Bat is both a mammal and a bird therefore, it inherits attributes and behaviors form both parents.

```
class Mammal { };
class Bird{ };
class Bat : Mammal, Bird{ };
```

49. How inheritance is specified?
See (Q9 & 48).

50. How multiple inheritance is specified?
See (Q48).

51. How to resolve conflicts in naming between multiple parent classes if they are called from a child?
- Derived class redefines the multiply-defined function in parents or,
- Derived class invokes member function in a particular base class using scope resolution operator ::
- Compiler errors occur if derived class uses base class function without one of above solutions.

52. What is code reuse?
It is a mechanism in OOP that facilitates the utilization of previously created code; its main advantages include: time saving, better resource utilization and reducing redundancy. One good example of code reuse is inheritance.

53. What is class extension?
It means inheritance; where a derived class inherits all of the base class content and extends the data member or/and the function members. In OOP inheritance implies extension where, there is no point of just inheriting the same content of the base class and not adding any data or function members, if that is the case then, the base class by itself could be used directly and no need for inheritance.

54. Define class aggregation
- Utilizing (by instantiation) one or more classes within another class to model a certain more complex object.
- Example: aggregating two instances of Point3D to model a line segment class.

```
#include "Point3D.h"
class Line3D{
private:
        Point3D p1;
        Point3D p2;

public:
        Line3D(void);
        ~Line3D(void);
        void setP1(Point3D& p);
        void setP2(Point3D& p);
        void print();
        double length();
};
```

55. Define nested classes
- Declaring and defining an inner class within another.
- Example:

```
//--------------- Point.h ---------------
class Point{
private:
public:
    class NestedClass{
    public:
        NestedClass(){ cout << " Example on class nesting ...\n"; }
    };
};

//------------------------- main.cpp -------------------
Point::NestedClass nc1;
```

56. When child class default constructor/destructor are called, what happens to parent?
- Default constructor: the parent constructor is called then the child's.
- Destructor: the child destructor is called first then the parent's.
- Typical as a demo, debugging messages are placed in default constructer and destructor to show this behavior.

57. When child class overloaded constructor are called what happens to parent?
- Parent's overloaded constructor is not called

58. How can an overloaded constructor of a parent class be called by its children?
- In the header of the overloaded constructor of the child, use ":" and issue a call to the parent overloaded constructor using the parameters (all or as needed) of child as the arguments to the parent's.
- The base class takes care of constructing its part of the data and the derived class takes care of its extended part only.
- Example:

```
//------------------ Point3D.cpp -------------------------
Point3D::Point3D(double x, double y, double z) : Point(x,y){
    This->z = z;
}
```

59. How polymorphism can be demonstrated?
Two ways:
- Using reference variables:

```
//---------------------- main.cpp -------------------------
void printObj(Point& p){
    p.print();
}
```

```
int main(){
    Point3D p0;
    Point p1 = p0;
    printObj( p1 );    // this will print the Point3D object
    return 0;
}
```

- Using pointer variables:
```
//------------------------ main.cpp ------------------------
void printObj(Point* p){
    p->print();
}
int main(){
    Point* p0 = new Point3D();
    printObj( p1 );    // this will print the Point3D object
    return 0;
}
```

NOTE: p0 is a pointer to Point but not a pointer to Point3D, so it ONLY can dereference members in Point but not those extended in derived classes. For example, the following statement is invalid: p0->setZ(1.2);

60. Define operator overloading
- For the language intrinsic data types such as {bool, char, short, int, etc.} the language defines all of their related operators such as {+, -, *, &&, ||, !, etc.}. As for the user defined data types (UDT), the designer of these classes must provide specific implementation of all required operators that can operate on a particular UDT. For example if a new data type was created for matrices then, what would the {+, -, *, /, etc. } mean for it.
- Example:
Let us implement an overloaded "-" operator for the Point class we have. The "-" operator for this class should mean the Euclidian distance between two points in 2D space and not simply subtracting two quantities.

```
//-------------------- Point.h --------------------
public:
double operator-(Point& p2);

//------------------- Point.cpp --------------------
double Point::operator-(Point& p2){
    return sqrt( pow(x-p2.x,2) + pow(y-p2.y,2) );
}
//---------------- main.cpp --------------------
Point p1(55.0, 33.0);
Point p2(22.0, 11.0);
cout << p1 - p2 << endl;    // =  39.6611
```

61. Define function templates
- A feature in c++ that enables functions to process any data type (intrinsic or UDT) as long as all the operations in the function template are defined for the data type to be processed. Without templates, the programmer needs to write a separate function for each data type.
- Example: a template swap function that would swap any two objects that have the "=" operator defined for them.

```cpp
template <class T>
void tswap( T& obj1, T& obj2 ){
    T temp = obj1;
    obj1 = obj2;
    obj2 = temp;
}


//---------------------- main.cpp ---------------------
int n1=99, n2=11;
tswap(n1, n2);
double d1=22.0, d2=33.0;
tswap(d1, d2);
Point p1(11.0, 99.0, new int[8]);
Point p2(22.0, 77.0, new int[8]);
tswap(p1, p2); // given that the "=" operator is defined in
Point class.
```

62. Define class templates
- Extends the concept of function templates as in (Q61) to class templates where the entire class can be generic and handles any data type as long as all used operations in the class templates are defined for these data types.
- Example: we'll create a simple TArray class that can store any data type.

```cpp
//----------------------- TArray.h --------------------------------
template<class T>
class TArray
{

private:
    T * A;
    int size;
public:
    TArray(void);
    TArray(int size);
    ~TArray(void);
    T min();
};
```

```
template<class T>
void TArray<T>::TArray(){
    size = 1024;
    A = new T[ size ];
    for( int i=0; i<size; ++i)
        A[i] = 0;
}

template<class T>
T TArray<T>::min(){
    T m = A[0];
    for(int i=0; i<size; ++i){
        if( A[i] < m )
            m = A[i];
    }
    return m;
}
```

63. What is exception handling?
- Is a construct and a mechanism that manages the occurrence of errors/abnormalities at run time. Exception handling is designed to separate the error handling code from the original code to gracefully handle the fault situation by transferring the program control to the exception handling code. Many aspects of software development process can be improved such as: safety, readability, writeability, maintainability, etc.
- Examples of exceptions: Divide by zero, sqrt of a negative, un initialized variable, exceeding array limits, dereferencing a dangling pointer, etc.

64. How and where is "throw" used?
- Any function can declare that it "throws" a certain type of an exception either defined in <exception> or a UDT, or it can leave the type empty in the "throw()" which indicates that it will throw any type of exception.
- Example:

```
double reciprocal(double x){
    if(x==0)
        throw std::overflow_error(" --- invalid operation --- ");
    else
        return 1/x;
}
int main(){
    try{
        cout << reciprocal(0);
    }
    catch(std::overflow_error e){
        cout << e.what() << endl;
    }
    return 0;
}
```

65. How multiple exceptions are handled?
- By using multiple "catch" blocks for the same "try" block.
- Example:

```
try{
    // ...
}
catch( std::overflow_error e ){
    // handle overflow
    cout << e.what();
}
catch( std::bad_alloc e ){
    // handle bad mem allocation
    cout << e.what();
}
catch( std::bad_cast e ){
    // handle bad dynamic cast
    cout << e.what();
}
catch( ... ){
    // handle default exception (the else case)
}
```

66. How and where try-catch blocks are used?
- If a certain code has a possible exception, it is placed within a "try" block where the code should be throwing that particular exception using "throw"; the "catch" block is used after the "try" block to handle one or more exceptions; use the catch(...) to catch default exception. See (Q64 & Q65).

67. In exception handling, how and why inner/customized classes are used?
- When the situation needs more than the standard exception types, the programmer can create her own classes to manage these new types. See the next example.
- Example: create an exception class to handle "index out of bound" error for the XArray class.

```
//-------------------- XArray.h --------------------------
template<class T>
class XArray{
private:
    T * A;
    int size;
public:
    XArray(void);
    XArray(int size);
    ~XArray(void);
    class IndexOutOfBound{
        public:
            void print(){ cout << "XArray<T>::[] index out of
                                bounds\n\n";}
    }; };
```

```
//----------------------- main.cpp -----------------------
XArray<double> myAD(16);
try{
    cout << " A[-5]    = " << setw(6) << myAD[-5] << endl;
}
catch(XArray<double>::IndexOutOfBound e){
    e.print();
}
```

68. Define hierarchical inheritance
- It is an inheritance structure where multiple classes are derived from one base as well as multi-level inheritance; meaning that any derived class can have other derived classes.
- General example: living being (base) → {animal, plant}. Animal → {mammal, bird, fish, reptile, amphibian}. So, a snake would be a reptile which is an animal which is a living being.

```
class LivingBeing{
};

class Animal : LivingBeing{
};

class Reptile : Animal{
};
```

69. Define inheritance modes
- The base class access specifier that gives different privileges to the derived class; placed right before the base class name in the inheritance statement. If no access specifier is found, it defaults to be "private". The following table summarizes these different cases:

Members in Base Class	Derivation Mode	Members become in Derived Class
Private	ANY	Inaccessible
Protected or Public	Protected	Protected
Protected or Public	Public	Same as Base Class

- Example: if Point3D wants to inherit from Point using public mode then: Point3D should be defined as follows:

```
class Point3D : public Point{

}
```

- As an important observation on this issue, the base class must declare its "private" section as "protected" if it intends to make it accessible by the derived classes.

70. Define shallow vs. deep copy

- *Shallow copy:* is automatically provided by the system when copying an old object to a newly created one using the copy constructor which does member-wise assignment. If all members are statically defined (no dynamic memory allocation) then, the shallow copy is safe and effective otherwise, the pointers to dynamic memory in both objects will be aliases and will point to the same location which is undesirable since objects are typically independent.
- Deep copy: solves the problem of shallow copy by allocating new independent memory for any dynamically allocated data in the copy constructor.
- Example: the "connectedTo" array/pointer in the Point class

Version 1: shallow copy
```
Point::Point( Point& p ){  // shallow copy constructor
    x=p.x;
    y=p.y;
    connectedTo = p.connectedTo;
}
```

Version 2: deep copy
```
Point::Point( Point& p ){  // DEEP copy constructor
    x=p.x;
    y=p.y;
    connectedTo = new int[MAX_CONN];
    for(int i=0; i<MAX_CONN; ++i) connectedTo[i] = p.connectedTo[i];
}
```

71. Define static data members

- They are data members defined with "static" key word. These data members become class members; they do not belong to an object but to the class; they can be accessed without the need to instantiate an object; they can be accessed using the class name and the scope resolution operator "::".
- A static data member can only be accessed from a static function member in the class.
- Example: define a static data member that keeps track of number created objects off of the Point class. See (Q72 - Q74) to see how they can be accessed.

```
// ---------------------- Point.h ------------------------
protected:
static int nObjs;
```

72. Define Static function members

- They are function members defined with "static" key word. These function members become class members; they do not belong to an object but to the class; they can be accessed without the need to instantiate an object; they can be accessed using the class name and the scope resolution operator "::".
- Example: define a static function member that keeps track of number created objects off of the Point class. See (Q72 - Q74) to see how they can be accessed.
- Observe in Point.cpp that we needed to update all constructors to increment nObjs every time a new object is created. We show only the default constructor but this should be reflected in

all other constructors. As for the destructor, we need to decrement nObj (--nObj) since an object will be destroyed.

```
// ------------------------- Point.h -------------------------
public:
static int getNobjs();

// ------------------------- Point.cpp -------------------------
int Point::getNobjs(){
    return nObjs;
}

Point::Point(){
    id = 0;
    size = 1;
    x = -1;
    y = -1;
    z = -1;
    nConnect = 8;
    connectedTo = new int[nConnect];
    ++nObjs;
}
```

73. How static data member can be accessed using an object?
- Two versions are shown below: using an object and direct access via a static function member.

```
//------------------------- main.cpp -------------------------
Point p0;
cout << " NObjs = " << p0.getNobjs() << endl;
cout << " NObjs = " << Point3D::getNobjs() << endl;
```

74. How static data member can be accessed without using an object?
- See (Q73).

75. What is class variable?
- They are static data members (See Q71).

76. What is object variable?
- They are all other non-static data members.

77. How do you initialize a class variable?
- Anywhere outside the class specification body, typically in the "class.cpp" implementation file. They are accessed using the class name and the scope resolution and set to appropriate values.

- They can be initialized within class specification body only if they are constants "static const".
- Example: initialize the static data member "nObjs" in Point class.

```
// ---------------------- Point.cpp ------------------------------
int Point3D::nObjs = 0;
```

78. How do you initialize an object variable?
- They only can be initialized in the implementations of the public interface functions in the implementation code: constructors, private functions and any other member functions of the class.
- Example: all data members are initialed in the default constructor of Point class.

```
// ------------------------------ Point.cpp --------------------
Point::Point(){
    id = 0;
    size = 1;
    clr = BLACK;
    x = -1;
    y = -1;
    z = -1;
    nConnect = 8;
    connectedTo = new int[nConnect];
    ++nObjs;
}
```

79. Explain stale data (meaning and solution)
- It is a situation where an output data is computed from an old input data although the user has fed her fresh data but, due to unreliable data handling in the class, the computation of the out data was erroneous.
- Example: in Point class assume that we have the two functions: void computeDist() ad double getDist(), follow the scenario in main.cpp. After line# 5, the user should've called computeDist() again and every time any input data changes in general.
- To avoid stale data, make sure the code that computes the needed output uses most recent input data. Do not separate compute and get in two functions, need to combine them in one, so every time the user need the output, it is actually recomputed not simply returned as in the scenario below.

```
//------------------------- Point.cpp --------------------------
void Point::computeDist(Point& p2){
    dist = sqrt( pow(p2.x-x,2) + pow(p2.y-y,2));
}

double getDist(){
    return dist;
}
```

```
//--------------------- main.cpp --------------------------
Point p1(11, 22);
Point p2(55, 66);
p1.computeDist( p2 );
cout << p1.getDist();      // will print 62.2254
p1.setX(88);
cout << p1.getDist();      // will print 62.2254 → stale data
```

80. How passing objects by value, by reference and as a pointer work?
- Create a printObj function with three versions to demonstrate the three cases:

```
//----------------------- main.cpp ------------------------
void printObj(Point p){
     p.print();
}

void printObj(Point& p){
     p.print();
}

void printObj(Point* p){
     p->print();
}

int main(){
     Point p1;
     Point* pp = &p1;
     printObj( p1 );     // works for the two functions val and &
     printObj( pp );      // works for the pointer parameter
function
}
```

81. How, where and why "const" keyword in the public interface?
- It is recommended to be used in all functions (especially the accessor functions) that do not intend to change any class data member to prevent accidental change to these data members. It is placed after the header of the function.
- Example: see (Q1) for getX() function in Point class.

82. In polymorphism, explain the "is-a" relation.
- Polymorphism is a mechanism that allows behaviors defined in base class to be dynamically bound to the appropriate behaviors in derived classes. To do that, only derived object/pointer can be assigned to base object/pointer but not vice versa, which is the essence of "is-a" relation since a child class "is-a" parent class is always valid such as a Point3D is a Point but we cannot say that a Point is a Point3D.
- Example:

```
Point* p1 = new Point3D(); // works
Point3D* p2 = new Point(); // syntax error
```

```
Point p3 = *p2;          // works
Point3D p4 = *p1;        // syntax error
```

83. For a template function to work, what are the conditions of the supported classes?

- All operators applied to the objects of the classes used in the function template must be supported in their classes.
- Example: see (Q61).

84. Why a template class must be written in one single file?

- By separating .h and .cpp files we hide the class implementation from its specification. Then, the implementation file can be compiled as an Obj code which a user can link it to her code. The user code must include the specification file ".h" file to be able to compile before linking.
- In non-template classes, all variables are defined as specific data types in .h and .cpp files. Therefore, compiler can generate the target machine code since the information of the data types is known.
- As for Template classes, no information about the specific data types are known in the template class in both sections specification and implementation. Only after the user instantiates an object as in:
                    TClass<int> myObj;
- After this instantiation statement, the complier can generate the specific version of the template class to match the specified data type(s).
- Due to all of the above, the template class must keep the specification and implementation sections in one file as source code. The implementation section can NOT be separately compiled into an .obj file to be linked with the user code.

85. Explain memory leakage

- Occurs when the programmer repeatedly allocates dynamic memory and does not release it when it is no longer needed, this will eventually exhaust all memory resources and cause a fatal error that will crash the program.
- Example: in version one the function keeps allocating memory for about 10GB, if the system has that space available, it would work but with a lot of wasted space. Version-2 correctly and safely releases the allocated memory after it has finished using it and will use 100MB at any given time.

```
// ------------------- main.pp -----------------------------------
for(int i=0; i<100; ++i)
    allocMem();

// ----------------- version-1 memory leakage --------------------
int allocMem(){
    int* p = new int[100000000];
    // process the array
    // return result
}
```

```
// -------------------- version-2 memory safe --------------------
int allocMem(){
    int* p = new int[100000000];
    // process the array
    // return results
    delete [] p;
}
```

86. How cascaded operators work?

- In applying multiple instances of the same operator in one statement where every result of one operator feeds into the next, the implementation of this overloaded operator in a class need to address this feature for the cascading to work.
- Example: if the "=" operator is required to support cascaded calls, it needs to return the current object as a result of the assignment operation so the next "=" in the statement can assign it to the operators left object so it can support this situation:

```
//---------------------- main.cpp ----------------------
Point p1(11, 22);
Point p2, p3, p4;
p4 = p3 = p2 = p1;

// the copy(p2) call in this operator: is a private function
// that copies passed object to this object
Point3D Point3D::operator=(Point3D& p2){
    copy(p2);
    return *this;
}
```

87. How to test a default constructor?

- The default constructor is called in two situations: when declaring an object and when creating a dynamic object using default constructor.
- Example:

```
// ---------------------- main.cpp ----------------------
Point p1; // calls default constructor
Point* p2 = new Point(); // calls default constructor
```

88. How to test a copy constructor?

- A copy constructor is called when copy constructor is explicitly called or an object is returned by value.
- Example:

```
Point p1(11, 22);    // overloaded constructor is called
Point p2( p1 );      // copy constructor is called
```

89. How to test a cascaded assignment operator?
- See (Q86)

90. How to create an array of objects derived from a common base class?

```
// using static array of objects
Point p1, p2, p3;
Point pal[3] = {p1, p2, p3};

// using dynamic array
Point* pa2 = new Point[3];
pa2[0] = p1;
pa2[1] = p2;
pa2[2] = p3;

for(int i=0; i<3; ++i){
    cout << pal[i].getX() << "\t";
    cout << pa2[i].getY() << endl;
}
```

91. What is a scope resolution operator mean?
- The "::" is used to identify which data/functions members belong to which class. It can be used in different situations:
  - o In a derived class to access the base class's members:
    ```
    // ----------------- Point3D.cpp -------------------
    Point3D(double x, double y, double z){
        Point::x = x;
        Point::y = y;
        This->z = z;
    }
    ```
  - o In main.cpp to access a static function:
    ```
    // --------------- main.cpp --------------------
    cout << Point::getNObj();
    ```

  - o Accessing an inner class with a main class:
    See (Q67).

92. How parent member functions can be accessed?
- Using the scope resolution operator "::".
- Example: if a child "print" function needs to call parent's "print" function first then:
```
// ------------------- Point3D.cpp -----------------
void Point3D::print(){
    Point::print();      // prints x, defined in parent
    cout << " Z-coord = " << z <<endl; // prints new data "z"
}
```

93. Can an object be returned from a stand-alone function, how?

- C++ allows objects to be returned form functions.
- Example: assume that we want to write a function that reads data members in a Point3D object, we could have this function to do that:

```cpp
// ------------------ main.cpp ------------------
Point3D readPoint(){
    Point3D p;
    cin >> p.x >> p.y >> p.z;
    return p;
}

// ------------- main() --------------------
Point3D p = readPoint();
```

94. Can an object be returned from its own methods, how?

- C++ has a feature that allow that; through the "this" key work an object can return itself in two ways:
  - o Returning a copy of itself
    ```cpp
    Point Point::getAcopy(){
        return *this;
    }
    ```

  - o Returning a pointer to the object
    ```cpp
    Point* Point::getAptr(){
        return this;
    }
    ```

```cpp
// ---------- main.cpp --------------------
Point p1, p2, *p3;

p2 = p1.getAcopy();
p2.setX(99);

p3 = p1.getAptr();
p3->setX(99);
```

95. Can a pointer to an object be returned from its own methods, how?

- See (Q94).

96. Can an array of objects be returned from a stand-alone function, how?

- Using dynamic memory allocation and returning a pointer to it.
- Example: assume that we want to create an array of Point and set x, y to passed parameters.

```cpp
// ------------------- main.cpp ------------------
```

```
Point* createPointArray( int size, double x, double y ){
    Point* pa = new Point[ size ];
    for(int i=0; i<size; ++i){
        pa[i].setX(x);
        pa[i].setY(y);
    }

    return pa;
}
```

97. What is a forward declaration, give an example?

- In situations where a class needs to use the name of another external class, a forward declaration statement is needed for the compiler to know that a class with this name exists outside this file. A typical situation is when defining a friend function of class A in class B, Class B needs a forward declaration statement of class A. The forward declaration statement in this case would be:

```
// ---------------------- Class_B.h ------------------------
class Class_A;
```

- See (Q38).

98. What is a circular reference/dependency among classes?

- It occurs when two classes declare each other in their header files so they depend on each other for their specifications to be complete, in this case forward declaration helps to solve the problem:
- Example: the first version shows circular dependency and the second version adds the forward declaration in both header files to solve the problem.

Version 1: circular dependency
```
//---------------------- Class_A.h ------------------------
class Class_A{
    Class_B var_B;
}
```

```
//---------------------- Class_B.h ------------------------
class Class_B{
    Class_A var_A;
}
```
Version 2: circular dependency solved by forward declaration
```
//---------------------- Class_A.h ------------------------
class B;
class Class_A{
    Class_B var_B;
}
```

```
//---------------------- Class_B.h ------------------------
class A;
```

```
class Class_B{
    Class_A var_A;
}
```

99. How to prevent multiple inclusions of the same header file in a project?
- The following directives will prevent multiple inclusions of a header file:

```
#ifndef MY_HEADER_H
#define MY_HEADER_H
// my header file
#endif
```

100.   Why it is recommended to make base class destructors virtual
- In normal situation they need not be virtual but in case of pointer to base is set to point to a derived object as in:

```
class Base{
    Base(){};
    ~Base(){};
}

class Derived{
    Derived(){};
    virtual ~Derived(){};
}

int main(){
    Base* p = new derived();
    Delete p;
}
```

Which destructor will be called? If the destructor in Base is not virtual, of course the base since the destructor of Base is statically bound but, if it is virtual, then the Derived version of destructor will be called.